HOUSEHOLD
POLISH
PHRASEBOOK

Other Books in the Series

HOME MAID SPANISH
by Margaret Storm and Elsie Ginnett

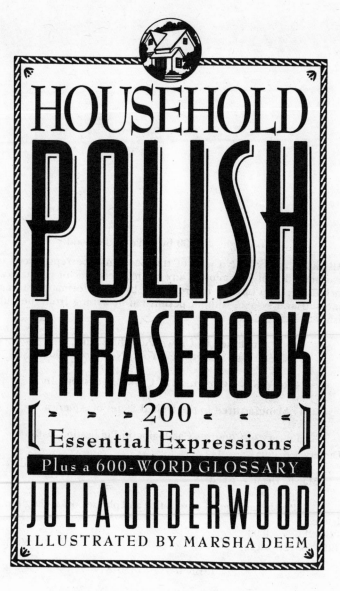

HOUSEHOLD POLISH PHRASEBOOK

200 Essential Expressions
Plus a 600-WORD GLOSSARY

JULIA UNDERWOOD
ILLUSTRATED BY MARSHA DEEM

CROWN PUBLISHERS, INC.
New York

Published by Crown Publishers, Inc.,
201 East 50th Street, New York, New York 10022

CROWN is a trademark of Crown Publishers, Inc.

Manufactured in the United States of America

Library of Congress Cataloging-in-Publication Data
Underwood, Julia.
    Household Polish phrasebook/Julia Underwood; illustrated by Marsha Deem.—1st ed.
        p. cm.
    1. Polish language—Conversation and phrase books—English.
I. title.
PG6121.U47   1990
491.8'583421—dc20   89-71213

ISBN 0-517-57426-8

10 9 8 7 6 5 4 3 2 1

First Edition

Contents

Polish Pronunciation Guide 3

Cardinal Numbers 6

Months 8

Days of the Week 9

Seasons 10

Public Holidays 10

Colors 11

Daily Expressions 12

First Day 14

Living Room 17

Bedroom 19

Kitchen 23

Bathroom 27

Laundry Room 29

Family Room 33

Child Care 35

Vocabulary 39

HOUSEHOLD

POLISH

PHRASEBOOK

POLISH PRONUNCIATION GUIDE

This booklet is written in a simplified form for people with no knowledge of Polish. English transcriptions in parentheses show how to pronounce each Polish word or phrase.

One letter of the alphabet usually corresponds to one sound in Polish spelling. However, some sounds are marked by a combination of two letters: ch, cz, dz, dź, dž, ńi, rz, sz. Others are indicated by letters of the alphabet with diacritical (accent) marks: ą, ć, ę, ó, ś, ź, ż.

The letters q, v, and x are not included in the Polish alphabet. The letter v is used occasionally in the booklet for simplification or for the pronunciation of the letter w. The following consonant sounds are pronounced as in English: b, d, f, k, l, m, n, p, s, t, z. The others are given below.

Polish Letter	Symbol	Example
a as u in hut	<u>a</u>	**sala** (sala) hall
ą as French *on*, nasal	<u>on</u>	**mąż** (monz) husband
c as ts in cats	<u>ts</u>	**córka** (tsoorka) daughter
ć,ci very soft ch	<u>ch</u>	**dać** (dach) give
ch as h in have	<u>h</u>	**chleb** (hleb) bread

cz as in church	<u>ch</u>	**czarny** (<u>ch</u>ar-ni) <u>bl</u>ack
dź as in ds in foods	<u>dz</u>	**bardzo** (bar<u>dz</u>o) very
dz as dg in budge	<u>dg</u>	**dziadek** (<u>dg</u>adek) grandfather
e as in led	<u>e</u>	**mleko** (mleko) mil<u>k</u>
ę nasal as in hen	<u>en</u>	**prędko** (pr<u>en</u>dko) qui<u>ck</u>ly
g as in go	<u>g</u>	**garnek** (<u>g</u>arnek) pot
h as in hen	<u>h</u>	**hotel** (<u>h</u>otel) hotel
i as in marine	<u>ee</u>	**pani** (pan<u>ee</u>) lady
j as y in yes	<u>y</u>	**jajko** (<u>y</u>a<u>y</u>ko) egg
ł as w in want	<u>w</u>	**sałata** (sa<u>w</u>ata) lettuce

4

ńi as ni in onion	<u>ny</u>	**wiśnia** (veesh<u>ny</u>a) cherry
o as in or	<u>o</u>	**okno** (<u>o</u>kn<u>o</u>) window
ó as oo in zoo	<u>oo</u>	**córka** (ts<u>oo</u>rka) daughter
r is trilled	<u>r</u>	**raczek** (<u>r</u>achek) shrimp
rz as sh in shed	<u>sh</u>	**przed** (p<u>sh</u>ed) before
rz as z in zip	<u>z</u>	**grzyb** (g<u>z</u>ib) mushroom
ś,si very soft sh	<u>sh</u>	**śiedem** (<u>sh</u>edem) seven
sz as sh in shot	<u>sh</u>	**szafa** (<u>sh</u>afa) cupboard
u as oo in zoo	<u>oo</u>	**ulica** (<u>oo</u>leetsa) street
w as v in van	<u>v</u>	**woda** (<u>v</u>oda) water
y as i in sit	<u>i</u>	**syn** (s<u>i</u>n) son
ż as z in zero	<u>z</u>	**żaba** (<u>z</u>aba) frog
z very soft s as in please	<u>zh</u>	**zima** (<u>zh</u>eema) winter

CARDINAL NUMBERS	KARDYNALNY NUMERY	(KAR-DI-NAL-NI NU-ME-RI)
0	zero	(zero)
1	jeden	(ye-den)
2	dwa	(dva)
3	trzy	(tshee)
4	cztery	(chte-ree)
5	pięc	(pyench)
6	sześć	(she-shch)
7	siedem	(she-dem)
8	osiem	(o-shem)
9	dziewięć	(dge-vyench)
10	dziesięć	(dge-shench)
11	jedenaście	(ye-de-nash-che)
12	dwanaście	(dva-nash-che)
13	trzynaście	(tshee-nash-che)
14	czternaście	(ch-ter-nash-che)
15	piętnaście	(pyent-nash-che)
16	szesnaście	(shes-nash-che)
17	siedemnaście	(she-dem-nash-che)
18	osiemnaście	(o-shem-nash-che)
19	dziewiętnaście	(dge-vyent-nash-che)
20	dwadzieścia	(dva-dgesh-cha)
21	dwadzieścia jeden	(dva-dgesh-chaye-den)

30	trzydzieści	(tshi-dgesh-chee)
40	czterdzieści	(chter-dgesh-chee)
50	pięcdzieśiąt	(pyench-dge-shont)
60	sześcdziesiąt	(sheshch-dge-shont)
70	siedemdziesiąt	(she-dem-dge-shont)
80	osiemdziesiąt	(oshem-dge-shont)
90	dziewięćdziesiąt	(dge-vyen-dge-shont)
100	sto	(sto)
200	dwieście	(dvyesh-che)
300	trzysta	(tshis-ta)
400	czterysta	(ch-ter-sta)
500	pięćset	(pyench-set)
600	sześćset	(she-shch-set)
700	siedemset	(she-dem-set)
800	osiemset	(oshem-set)
900	dziewięćset	(dge-vyench-set)
1000	tysiąc	(tish-onts)
1,000,000	milion	(meel-yon)

MONTHS	MIESIACY	(MYE-SHONTSY)
January	**styczen**	(sti-chen)
February	**luty**	(loo-ti)
March	**marzec**	(ma-zhets)
April	**kwiecień**	(kvye-chen)
May	**maj**	(may)
June	**czerwiec**	(cher-vyets)
July	**lipiec**	(lee-pyets)
August	**sierpień**	(sher-pyen)
September	**wrzesień**	(vzhe-shen)
October	**październik**	(pazh-dger-neek)
November	**listopad**	(lee-sto-pad)
December	**grudzień**	(groo-dgen)

DAYS OF THE WEEK	DNI W TYDZIEN	(DNEE V TI-DZHEN)
Sunday	**niedziela**	(nye-dge-la)
Monday	**poniedzałek**	(po-nye-dga-wek)
Tuesday	**wtorek**	(fto-rek)
Wednesday	**środa**	(shro-da)
Thursday	**czwartek**	(chvar-tek)
Friday	**piątek**	(pyon-tek)
Saturday	**sobota**	(so-bo-ta)

SEASONS	PORA ROKU	(PO-RA RO-KOO)
Spring	**wiosna**	(vyos-na)
Summer	**lato**	(la-to)
Autumn	**jesień**	(ye-shen)
Winter	**zima**	(zhee-ma)

PUBLIC HOLIDAYS	PUBLICZNY SWIĘNTA	(PUB-LEECH-NI SHVYEN-TA)
New Year	**Nowy Rok**	(no-vi rok)
Easter	**Wielkanoc**	(v-yel-ka-nots)
Christmas	**Boze Narodze- nie**	(bo-ze na-ro-dge- nye)

COLORS	KOLORY	(KO-LO-RI)
beige	**beżowy**	(be-zho-vi)
black	**czarny**	(char-ni)
blue	**niebieski**	(nye-byes-kee)
brown	**brązowy**	(bron-zo-vi)
gold	**złoty**	(zwo-ti)
green	**zielony**	(zhe-lo-ni)
gray	**szary**	(sha-ri)
mauve	**fiołkoworożowy**	(fyow-kovo-roo-zho-vi)
orange	**pomarańczowy**	(po-ma-ran-cho-vi)
pink	**różowy**	(roo-zho-vi)
purple	**purpurowy**	(poor-poo-ro-vi)
red	**czerwony**	(cher-vo-ni)
silver	**srebrny**	(sre-brni)
white	**biały**	(bya-wi)
yellow	**żółty**	(zhoow-ti)

DAILY EX- PRESSIONS	CODZIENNE WYRAZENIA	(TSO-DGENN-NE VI-RA-ZE-NYA)
Good morn- ing, hello	Dzień dobry	(dgen do-bri)
Good evening	Dobry wieczór	(do-bri vye-choor)
Good night	Dobranoc	(dob-ra-nots)
Good-bye	Do widzenia	(do vee-dze-nya)
Please	Proszę	(pro-shen)
Thank you	Dziękuje	(dgen-koo-ye)
You're wel- come	Proszę bardzo	(pro-shen bar-dzo)
Excuse me	Przepraszam	(pshe-pra-sham)
How do you do?	Jak się masz?	(Yak shen mash)
I don't un- derstand	Ja nie rozu- miem	(ya nye ro-zoo-myem)
Mister	Pan	(pan)
Mrs.	Pani	(pa-nee)
Miss	Panienka	(pa-nyenka)

What is your name?	**Jak się (Pan, Pani) nazywa?**	(Yak shen [Pan, pa-nee] na-zi-wa)
My name is . . .	**Nazywam się**	(na-zi-vam shen)
Where do you live?	**Gdzie (Pan, Pani) mieszka?**	(Gdze [Pan, Pa-nee] m-yesh-ka)
What is your phone number?	**Co jest (Pana, Pani) telefon numer?**	(Tso yest [Pa-na, Pa-nee] te-le-fon noo-mer)

FIRST DAY   PIERSZY DZIEN   (PYER-SHI DGEN)

What is your address?
Co jest wasz address?
(Tso yest vash a-dress)

How will you get here?
Jak Pani tutaj pszyjedzie?
(Yak Pa-nee too-tay pshe-ye-dge)

Will you be taking a train or a bus?
Czy Pani pszyjedzie pociągiem, czy autobusem?
(Tshi Pa-nee pshi-ye-dge po-chon-gém, tshi ou-to-bu-
    sem)

Will someone drive you?
Czy ktoś Pani Pszywiezie?
(Tshi k-tosh pa-nee pshi-v-ye-zhe)

Will you live in?
Czy pani będzie tutay mieszkać?
(Tshi pa-nee ben-dge too-tay m-yesh-kach)

You will begin working on _____ . (day)
Pani zacznie pracować _____ . (dzień)
(Pa-nee zash-nye pra-tso-vach)

You will begin working at _____ o'clock.
Pani zaczyna prace o _____ godzinie.
(Pa-nee za-chee-na pra-tse o _____ go-dgee-nye)

You will finish working at _____ o'clock.
Pani zkonczy pracować o _____ godzinie.
(Pa-nee s-kon-shi pra-tso-vach o _____ go-dgee-nye)

You can make your lunch from food in the refrigerator.
Pani może sobie zrobić obiad od jedzienie w lodown-icy.
(Pa-nee moze so-bye zro-beech ob-yad od ye-dze-nye v lo-dov-nee-tsi)

I am going shopping and will return at _____o'clock.
Ja idę na sprawunki i powróce o _____godzinie.
(Ya eeden na spra-voon-kee ee pov-roo-tse o _____go-dgee-nye)

You may use this room to change your clothes.
Pani może urzywać ten pokój się pszebierać.
(Pa-nee moze oo-zhi-vach ten po-kooy shen pshe-bye-rach)

You may hang your clothes in this closet.
Pani może powieszać swoje ubrania w tem gabinecie.
(Pa-nee moze po-vye-shach svoye oo-bra-nya v tem ga-bee-ne-che)

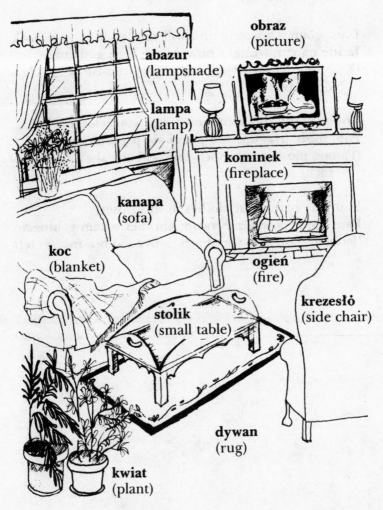

draperja
(drapes)

obraz
(picture)

abazur
(lampshade)

lampa
(lamp)

kominek
(fireplace)

kanapa
(sofa)

koc
(blanket)

ogień
(fire)

krzesło
(side chair)

stolik
(small table)

dywan
(rug)

kwiat
(plant)

LIVING ROOM POKÓY SALA (PO-KOOY SA-LA)

Please clean the living room.
Proszę poczyścić sale.
(Pro-shen po-chish-cheech sa-le)

Please clean the carpet and drapes with the vacuum cleaner.
Proszę wyczyścić dywan i draperje maszyna.
(Pro-shen vi-chish-cheech divan ee dra-per-ye mashi-non)

Please move the furniture and clean behind it.
Proszę wysuwiać meble i czyścić poza meblami.
(Pro-shen vi-soo-v-yach meb-le ee chish-cheech po-zha meb-la-mee)

Please dust the furniture and the pictures.
Proszę wycierać kurz od mebli i od obrazów.
(Pro-shen vi-chye-rach kooz od meb-lee ee od ob-ra-zoov)

Please dust the books and the bookcases.
Proszę wycierać kurz od ksiązków i bibljoteczki.
(Pro-shen vi-chye-rach kooz od kshonz-koov ee bib-lyo-tech-kee)

Please wax and polish the furniture.
Proszę woskować i pucować meble.
(Pro-shen vos-ko-vach ee poo-tso-vach meble)

Please clean, wax, and polish the floor.
Proszę wyczyścić, woskować, i pucować podłoge.
(Pro-shen vi-chish-cheech, vos-ko-vach, ee poo-tso-vach
podwoge)

Please wax and polish the piano but not the keys.
**Proszę woskować i pucować fortepian ale nie klawja-
ture.**
(Pro-shen vos-ko-vach ee poo-tso-vach for-tep-yan ale
nye kla-vya-toore)

Please wash the windows.
Proszę umyć okna.
(Pro-shen vi-mich ok-na)

Please clean the ashes from the fireplace.
Proszę wyczyćić popioł z komina.
(Pro-shen vi-chish-cheech pop-yuw z ko-mee-na)

This is very valuable, please be careful.
To jest bardzo wartościowe, proszę uwarżać.
(To yest bar-dgo var-tosh-cho-ve, pro-shen oo-va-zach)

BEDROOM   SYPIALNIA   (SI-PYAL-NYA)

Please clean the bedroom and make the bed.
Proszę wyczyścić sepialnie i poskładać łóż-ko.
(Pro-shen vi-chish-cheech sep-yal-nye ee pos-kwa-dach woozh-ko)

Please change the sheets and pillowcases.
Proszę zmienić p6ześcieradło i poszewki.
(Pro-shen z-mye-neech pshesh-che-rad-wo ee po-shev-kee)

Please dust the furniture and wash the mirrors.
Proszę wyćierać kurz z meblach i wymyć lustro.
(Pro-shen vi-chye-rach kooz z meb-lah ee vi-mich loo-stro)

Please clean the closets.
Proszę wyczyścić gabinety.
(Pro-shen vi-chish-cheech ga-bee-neti)

Please vacuum the carpet.
Proszę wyczyścić dywan maszyną.
(Pro-shen vi-chish-cheech di-van ma-shi-non)

Please wax and polish the floor.
Proszę woskować i pucować podłoge.
(Pro-shen vos-ko-vach ee poo-tso-vach pod-wo-ge)

Please wash the curtains.
Proszę wyprać firanki.
(Pro-shen vi-prach fee-ran-kee)

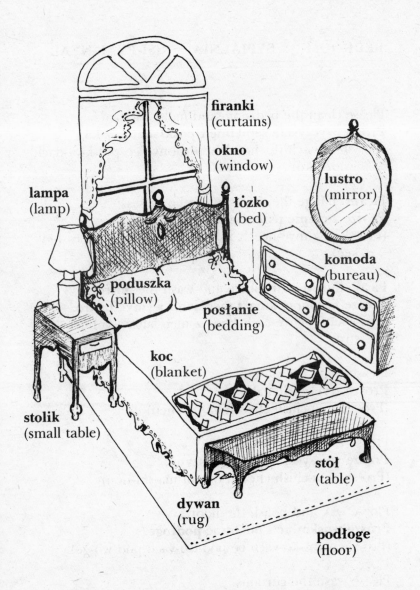

firanki
(curtains)

okno
(window)

lampa
(lamp)

łozko
(bed)

lustro
(mirror)

poduszka
(pillow)

komoda
(bureau)

posłanie
(bedding)

koc
(blanket)

stolik
(small table)

stół
(table)

dywan
(rug)

podłoge
(floor)

20

Please wash the linens from the bed.
Proszę wyprać bielizne z łuszka.
(Pro-shen vi-prach b-ye-leez-ne z woosh-ka)

Please wash the blanket and the quilt.
Proszę wyprać koc i kołdre.
(Pro-shen vi-prach kots ee kow-dre)

Please turn the mattress.
Proszę zwrócić materac.
(Pro-shen z-vroo-cheech ma-te-ras)

lodówka
(refrigerator)

gabinet
(cabinet)

ściek
(sink)

maszyna na talerzy
(dishwasher)

piec
(stove)

krezsło
(chair)

stół
(table)

podłoge
(floor)

KITCHEN   KUCHNIA   (KOOH-NYA)

Please clean the stove, the oven, and the burners on top.
Proszę wyćierać piec i palniki na wiszcha.
(Pro-shen vi-che-rach pyets ee pal-nee-kee na veesh-ha)

Please wash the refrigerator and the shelves inside.
Proszę wymyć lodówke i półki w sierodku.
(Pro-shen vi-mich lo-doov-ke ee pool-kee v she-rod-koo)

Please wash and polish the kitchen cupboards.
Proszę wymyć i pucować szafy w kuchni.
(Pro-shen vi-mich ee poo-tso-vach sha-fi v kooh-nee)

Please wash the cupboards inside and change the paper.
Proszę wymyć szafe w sierodku i zmienić papier.
(Pro-shen vi-mich sha-fe v she-rod-koo ee z-mye-neech
   pap-yer)

Please clean the sink and counters.
Proszę wymyć sćiek i kantor.
(Pro-shen vi-mich sh-check ee kan-tor)

Please take the trash into the large container outside.
Proszę wziąść śmiećie do durzey blaszanki na dworze.
(Pro-shen v-zon-sh sh-mye-che do doo-zey bla-shan-kee
   na dvo-she)

Please wash the garbage can and put a liner in it.
Proszę wymyć blaszanke i połorzyc torbe w śierodku.
(Pro-shen vi-mich bla-shan-ke ee po-wo-zich tor-be v
   she-rod-koo)

Please sweep and wash the kitchen floor.
Proszę zamiatać i wymyć podłoge w kuchni.
(Pro-shen za-myatach ee vi-mich pod-wo-ge v kooh-
    nee)

Please wax and polish the kitchen floor.
Proszę wymyć i pucować podłoge w kuchni.
(Pro-shen vi-mich ee poo-tso-vach pod-wo-ge v kooh-
    nee)

Please wash the table and chairs in the kitchen.
Proszę wymyć stół i krzesła w kuchni.
(Pro-shen vi-mich stoow ee kshe-swa v kooh-nee)

Please clean under the sink and replace the paper.
Proszę wymyć pod ściekiem i połorzyc nowy papier.
(Pro-shen vi-mich pod sh-check-em ee po-wo-zich pap-
    yer)

Please polish the silver.
Proszę pucować śrebrowe rzeczy.
(Pro-shen poo-tso-vach sh-reb-ro-ve ze-chi)

Please put the groceries away in the refrigerator and
    cupboards.
**Proszę połorzyc towary korzenne do lodówki i do
    szafy.**
(Pro-shen po-wo-zich to-va-ri ko-shen-ne do lo-doof-kee
    ee do sha-fi)

24

Please wash the fruits and vegetables thoroughly before
you put them away.

**Proszę wymyć jarzyny i owoce bardzo dobrze i
połorzyć do lodówki.**

(Pro-shen vi-mich ya-zi-ni ee o-vo-tse bar-dgo dob-ze ee
po-wo-zich do lo-doof-kee)

Please put these items in the freezer.

Proszę połorzyć te rzeczy do mrozicy.

(Pro-shen po-wo-zich te ze-chi do mro-zee-chi)

This is the automatic dishwasher.

To jest maszyna na talerzy.

(To yest ma-shi-na na ta-le-zi)

Please scrape and rinse the dishes before putting them
in the dishwasher.

**Proszę skrobać i płukać talerzy pszed myćiem w
maszynie.**

(Pro-shen sk-ro-bach ee pwoo-kach ta-le-zi pshed mi-
chem v ma-shi-nye)

Please use this special soap for the dishwasher.

Proszę urzywać te mydło tylko do maszyny na talerzy.

(Pro-shen oo-zi-vach te mid-wo til-ko do ma-shi-ni na
ta-le-zi)

Please turn the dishwasher on like this.

Proszę maszyne zaczynać w taki sposòb.

(Pro-shen ma-shi-ne za-chi-nach v ta-kee spo-soob)

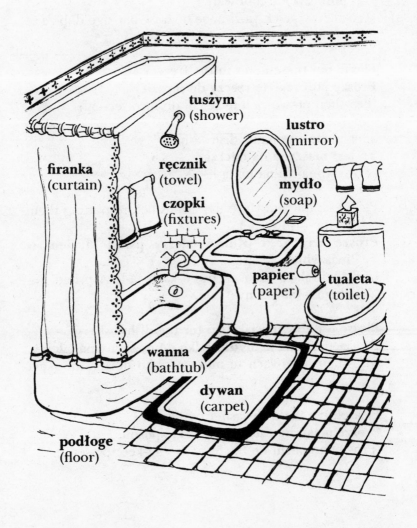

tuszym
(shower)

lustro
(mirror)

firanka
(curtain)

ręcznik
(towel)

czopki
(fixtures)

mydło
(soap)

papier
(paper)

tualeta
(toilet)

wanna
(bathtub)

dywan
(carpet)

podłoge
(floor)

BATHROOM   LAZIENKA   (WA-ZYEN-KA)

Please clean the toilet inside and out with this brush.
Proszę wymyć tualete w śierodku i nakoło tą szczotką.
(Pro-shen vi-mich twa-let v she-rod-koo ee na-ko-wo ton
  sh-chot-kon)

Please wash the bathtub, sink, and polish the fixtures.
Proszę wymyć wanne, śćiek, i pucować czopki.
(Pro-shen vi-mich van-ne, sh-check, ee poo-tso-vach
  chop-kee)

Please wash and polish the mirrors.
Proszę wymyć i pucować lustro.
(Pro-shen vi-mich ee poo-tso-vach loos-tro)

Please empty the hamper and put the clothes in the
  laundry room.
Proszę wypróźniać kosz i połorzyć bielizne do prania.
(Pro-shen vi-prooz-nyach kosh ee po-wo-zeech bye-leez-
  ne do pra-nya)

Please wash the shower walls and tile around the tub.
Proszę wymyć śćiany w tuszym i kafelki koło wanny.
(Pro-shen vi-mich shcha-ni v too-shim ee ka-fel-kee
  kowo van-ni)

Please wash the floor in the shower and in the bathroom.
Proszę wymyć podłoge w tuszym i w całey łazience.
(Pro-shen vi-mich pod-wo-ge v too-shim ee v tsa-wey
  wa-zyen-che)

Please wash and polish the shower door.
Proszę wymyć i pucować drzwi z tuszym.
(Pro-shen vi-mich ee poo-tso-vach dgvee z too-shim)

Please wash the towels and the shower curtain.
Proszę wyprać ręczniki i firanki z tuszym.
(Pro-shen vi-prach rench-nee-kee ee fee-ran-kee z too-
    shim)

Please put fresh soap in the soap dishes.
Proszę połorzyć nowe mydło do talerzy na mydło.
(Pro-shen po-wo-zeech no-ve mid-wo do ta-le-zi na
    mid-wo)

LAUNDRY ROOM   PRALNIA   (PRAL-NYA)

Please separate the laundry into white, colors, and dark.
Proszę oddzielić bielizne na białe, kolorowe, i ćiemne.
(Pro-shen od-dze-leech bye-leez-ne na bya-we, ko-lo-
ro-ve, ee chem-ne)

Please wash each pile of laundry separately in washer.
Proszę wyprać bielizne w maszynie tak jak oddzielona.
(Pro-shen vi-prach bye-leez-ne v mashi-nye tak yak
od-dze-lo-na)

Please put some bleach in with the white laundry.
Proszę polewać bielic do biały bielizny.
(Pro-shen po-le-vach bye-leech do bya-wi bye-leez-ni)

Please put the clothes in the dryer.
Proszę połorzyc bielizne do maszyny na wysuszenie.
(Pro-shen po-wo-zich bye-leez-ne do ma-shi-ni na vi-
soo-she-nye)

Please iron these clothes.
Proszę prasować tą bielizne.
(Pro-shen pra-so-wach ton bye-leez-ne)

Please use spray starch on these clothes.
Proszę połorzyc krochmal na tą bielizne.
(Pro-shen po-wo-zich kroch-mal na ton bye-leez-ne)

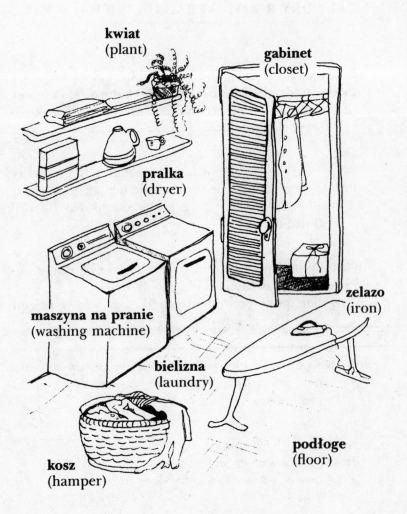

kwiat
(plant)

gabinet
(closet)

pralka
(dryer)

maszyna na pranie
(washing machine)

zelazo
(iron)

bielizna
(laundry)

podłoge
(floor)

kosz
(hamper)

Please fold the laundry, towels, and linens.
Proszę faldować bielizne, ręczniki, i przescieradła.
(Pro-shen fal-do-vach bye-leez-ne, rench-nee-kee, ee
  pshesh-che-rad-wa)

Please put the towels and the linens in the linen closet.
**Proszę połorzyć ręczniki, prześćieradła i poszewki do
szafy na bielizne.**
(Pro-shen po-wo-zeech rench-nee-kee, pshesh-che-rad-
  wo ee po-shev-kee do sha-fi na bye-leez-ne)

Please give these clothes to the man from the dry
  cleaners.
Proszę dać tą bielizne do męszczyzny na czyszczenia.
(Pro-shen dach ton bye-leez-ne do men-chiz-ni na chish-
  che-nya)

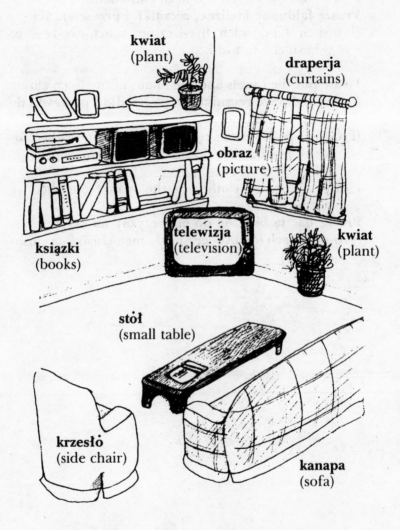

kwiat
(plant)

draperja
(curtains)

obraz
(picture)

książki
(books)

telewizja
(television)

kwiat
(plant)

stół
(small table)

krzesło
(side chair)

kanapa
(sofa)

FAMILY ROOM   RODZINNY   (RO-DZEEN-
                  POKÓJ   NI PO-KOOY)

Please dust the furniture and vacuum the rug.
Proszę pośćierać kuz z meblach i wyczyśćić dywan.
(Pro-shen pos-che-rach kooz z meb-lach ee vi-chish-
cheech di-van)

Please do not disturb the papers on the desk.
Proszę nie ruszać papiery na biurku.
(Pro-shen nye roo-shach pap-ye-ri na byoor-koo)

Please empty the wastebasket.
Proszę wypróznić kocz z smieći.
(Pro-shen vi-prooz-neech kots z sh-mye-chee)

Please pick up the children's toys and put them here.
Proszę pozbierać zabawki i połorzyc tutay.
(Pro-shen poz-bye-rach za-bav-kee ee po-wo-zich too-
tay)

Please put the magazines here.
Proszę połorzyć magazyny tutaj.
(Pro-shen po-wo-zich ma-ga-zi-ni too-tay)

Please dispose of the newspapers in the garage.
Proszę wyrzućić gazety do garaz.
(Pro-shen vi-zoo-cheech ga-ze-ti do ga-raz)

Please put the trash and newspapers in the bin outside.
Proszę wyrzućić gazety i smieći do blaszanki na dworze.
(Pro-shen vi-zoo-cheech ga-ze-ti ee shmye-chee do bla-shan-kee na dvo-ze)

Please dust the books and the bookshelves.
Proszę posćierać kurz z ksiązkach i z półkach.
(Pro-shen pos-che-rach kooz z kshon-zkah ee z poow-kah)

Please wash the ashtrays and the glass on the TV.
Proszę wymyć talerzy z popiołu i szkło na telewizji.
(Pro-shen vi-mich ta-le-zi z pop-yo-woo ee sh-kwo na te-le-veez-yee)

Please water all the plants in the house.
Proszę polewać kwiaty w całem domu.
(Pro-shen po-le-vach kvya-ti v tsa-wem do-moo)

CHILD CARE   OPIEKA   (OP-YEKA
                             DZIECKA   DGETS-KA)

The baby's name is _____ .
Dziecko się nazywa _____ .
(Dgets-ko shen na-zi-va)

My daughter's name is _____ .
Moja córka się nazywa _____ .
(Mo-ya tsoor-ka shen na-zi-va)

My son's name is _____ .
Mój syn się nazywa _____ .
(Mooy sin shen na-zi-va)

The clean diapers are kept here.
Czyste pieluchi są tutaj.
(Chis-te pye-loo-hee son too-tay)

Please put the soiled diapers here.
Proszę połorzyc brudne pieluchi tutaj.
(Pro-shen po-wo-zeech brood-ne pye-loo-hee too-tay)

These are disposable diapers.
To są pieluchi do wyrzucenia.
(To son pye-loo-hee do vi-zoo-tsen-ya)

Please feed the baby at _____and heat the bottle like this.
Proszę dać dziecko jedzenie o _____i zagrzać mleko tak.
(Pro-shen dach dgets-ko ye-dgen-ye o _____ee zag-zach mleko tak)

lampa
(lamp)

okno
(window)

lustro
(mirror)

komora
(crib)

koc
(blanket)

mleko
(milk)

krzesło
(high chair)

zabawki
(toys)

Give the baby soup, vegetables, egg, and fruit.
Proszę dać dziecko zupe, jarzyny, jajko, i owoce.
(Pro-shen dach dghets-ko zoo-pe, ya-zi-ni, yayko, ee
o-vo tse)

Please put the baby down for a nap at _____ .
Proszę połorzyc dziecko do spania o _____ .
(Pro-shen po-wo-zeech dzhets-ko do spa-nya o)

Give the children their lunch at _____ .
Proszę dać dzieciom obiad o _____godzinie.
(Pro-shen dach dge-chom ob-yad o _____go-dzee-nye)

The children will be home from school at _____ .
Dzieci będą w domu z szkoły o _____godzinie.
(Dge-chee ben-down v do-moo z sh-ko-wi o _____go-
dzee-nye)

Please give the children cookies and milk after school.
Proszę dać dziećom ćiastka i mleko po szkole.
(Pro-shen dach dge-chom chast-ka ee mle-ko po shko-le)

Please keep the children at home after school.
Proszę trzymać dzieci w domu po szkole.
(Pro-shen tshi-mach dge-chee v do-moo po shko-le)

Please have them do homework or watch TV.
Oni mają robić zadanie albo patrzyć na televisje.
(Onee ma-yon ro-beech za-da-nye al-bo pat-zich na
te-le-veesye)

Please give them dinner at _____o'clock.
Proszę im dać kolacje o _____godzinie.
(Pro-shen eem dach ko-lats-ye o _____go-dzee-nye)

Please give the children a bath before bedtime.
Proszę dać dzieći do kompielni pszed spaniem.
(Pro-shen dach dge-chee do kom-pyel-nee pshed spa-
nyem)

Please be sure they brush their teeth before bedtime.
**Proszę zauwarzyć ze oni wymyją zemby pszed span-
iem.**
(Pro-shen za-oo-va-zeech ze o-nee vi-mi-yon zem-bi p-
shed spa-nyem)

Please put them to bed at _____o'clock.
Proszę ich połorzyć do spania o _____godzinie.
(Pro-shen eeh po-wo-zeech do spa-nya o _____go-dzee-
nye)

If necessary, I can be reached at _____ .
Gdy, potrzebno, mnie zatelefonować do _____ .
(Gdi pot-sheb-no, mnye za-tele-fono-vach do)

The doctor's name is _____ , phone _____ .
Lekarz nazwisko jest _____ , telefon _____ .
(Lekaz na-zvee-sko yest _____ , te-le-fon)

VOCABULARY   SLOWNIK   (SWOVNIK)

about	**około**	(o-ko-wo)
afterward	**pózniej**	(pooz-nyey)
almost	**prawie**	(prav-ye)
although	**chociaz**	(ho-chazh)
apartment	**apartament**	(a-part-a-ment)
apple	**jablko**	(yap-ko)
apricot	**morela**	(mo-re-la)
apron	**fartuszek**	(far-too-shek)
arm	**ramie**	(ram-ye)
arrive	**przybywać**	(pshi-bi-vach)
ashes	**popioł**	(po-pyoow)
ashtray	**popielniczka**	(po-pyel-neech-ka)
asparagus	**szparag**	(shpa-rag)
aspirin	**aspiryna**	(as-pee-ri-na)
baby	**niemowlę**	(nye-mov-len)
back	**plecy**	(ple-tsi)
bacon	**słonina**	(swo-nee-na)
bad	**niedobry**	(nye-dob-ri)
bakery	**piekarnia**	(pye-kar-nya)
ball	**pilka**	(peel-ka)
banana	**banan**	(ba-nan)
bandage	**bandaz**	(ban-dazh)
bath	**kąpiel**	(kom-pyel)
bathtub	**wanna**	(van-na)
beach	**plaza**	(pla-zha)
beans	**fasola**	(fa-so-la)
beautiful	**piękny**	(pyen-kni)
because	**poniewaz**	(po-nye-vash)
bed	**łozko**	(wooz-ko)

39

bedding	**posłanie**	(pos-wa-nye)
bedroom	**sepialnia**	(sep-yal-nya)
bedtime	**pora do spania**	(po-ra do spa-nya)
beef	**wołowina**	(vo-wo-vee-na)
beer	**piwo**	(pee-vo)
beets	**buraki**	(boo-ra-kee)
before	**przed**	(pshed)
behave	**zachowywać sie**	(zo-ho-vi-vach shen)
bell	**dzwoń**	(dzvon)
belly	**brzuch**	(bzooh)
beneath	**pod**	(pod)
best	**najlepszy**	(nay-lep-shi)
between	**między**	(myen-dzi)
bib	**podbrodek**	(pod-bro-dek)
bicycle	**rowek**	(ro-vek)
big	**durzy**	(doo-zi)
bill	**rachunek**	(ra-hoo-nek)
bird	**ptak**	(p-tak)
birthday	**urodziny**	(oo-ro-dzee-ni)
bite	**ukąszyć**	(oo-kon-shich)
bitter	**gorzki**	(goz-kee)
black	**czarny**	(char-ni)
blanket	**koc**	(kots)
bleach	**bielić**	(bye-leech)
blond	**blondyn**	(blon-din)
blood	**krew**	(krev)
blouse	**bluzka**	(bloos-ka)
blue	**niebieski**	(nye-byes-kee)
board	**deska**	(des-ka)
bone	**kość**	(kosh-ch)
book	**ksiązka**	(kshonz-ka)
bookcase	**półka na ksiąszki**	(poow-ka na kshon-shkee)
both	**oboje**	(o-bo-ye)
bottle	**butelka**	(boo-tel-ka)
bottom	**spód**	(spood)

box	**pudełko**	(poo-dew-ko)
bread	**chleb**	(hleb)
breakfast	**sniadanie**	(shnya-da-nye)
broom	**miotła**	(myot-wa)
brush	**szczotka**	(sh-chot-ka)
bucket	**kubeł**	(koo-bew)
burn, to	**palić**	(pa-leech)
burners	**palniki**	(pal-nee-kee)
but	**ale**	(a-le)
butter	**masło**	(mas-wo)
button	**guzik**	(goo-zeek)
button, to	**zapinać**	(za-pee-nach)
cab	**dorózka**	(do-rooz-ka)
cabbage	**kapusta**	(ka-poos-ta)
cabinet	**gabinet**	(ga-bee-net)
cafe	**kawiarńia**	(kav-yar-nya)
cage	**klatka**	(klat-ka)
cake	**ćiastko**	(chast-ko)
calendar	**kalendarz**	(ka-len-dash)
call, to	**zawołać**	(za-vo-wach)
calm	**spokój**	(spo-kooy)
camp	**obóz**	(o-boos)
cancel	**kasować**	(ka-so-vach)
candle	**świeca**	(sh-vye-tsa)
candy	**ćokerki**	(tsoo-ker-kee)
canister	**puszka**	(poosh-ka)
canned	**konserwowany**	(kon-ser-vo-vani)
car	**automobil**	(ow-to-mo-beel)
card	**karta**	(kar-ta)
care, to take	**pielęgnować**	(pye-leng-no-vach)
carpet	**dywan**	(di-van)
carrot	**marchew**	(mar-hev)
carry	**nieść**	(nyesh-ch)
cart	**wóz**	(vooz)
carve	**krajać**	(kra-yach)

cat	**kot**	(kot)
catch, to	**złapać**	(zwa-pach)
cauliflower	**kalafior**	(ka-la-fyor)
celery	**salera**	(sa-le-ra)
cellar	**piwnica**	(peev-nee-tsa)
century	**stulećie**	(stoo-le-che)
certain	**pewny**	(pev-ni)
chair	**krzesło**	(kshes-wo)
chance	**traf**	(traf)
chandelier	**kandelabr**	(kan-de-labr)
change	**zmiana**	(z-mya-na)
chase	**gońić**	(go-neech)
cheery	**wisńia**	(veesh-nya)
cheese	**syr**	(sir)
chest, body	**piersi**	(pyer-shee)
chest of drawers	**komoda**	(ko-mo-da)
chicken	**kura**	(koo-ra)
child	**dziecko**	(dzets-ko)
children	**dzieći**	(dze-chee)
chimney	**komin**	(ko-meen)
chin	**broda**	(bro-da)
chive	**szczepiorek**	(sh-che-pyo-rek)
chocolate	**czekolada**	(che-ko-la-da)
choice	**wybór**	(vi-boor)
choke	**duśić**	(doo-sheech)
church	**kościół**	(kosh-choow)
chute	**rynna**	(rin-na)
cinnamon	**cynamon**	(tsi-na-mon)
circle	**koło**	(ko-wo)
circus	**cyrk**	(tsirk)
citizen	**obywatel**	(o-bi-va-tel)
city	**miasto**	(myas-to)
class	**klasa**	(kla-sa)
clatter	**stukot**	(stoo-kot)
clean	**czysty**	(chis-ti)
clear	**jasny**	(yas-ni)

climate	klimat	(klee-mat)
climb	wspinać	(vspee-nach)
clock	zegar	(ze-gar)
close, to	zamknąć	(zam-knonch)
closet	gabinet	(ga-bee-net)
cloth	materjał	(ma-ter-yaw)
clothes	ubranie	(oo-bra-nye)
cloud	chmura	(hmoo-ra)
coat	marynarka	(ma-ri-nar-ka)
coffee	kawa	(ka-va)
cold	zimno	(zeem-no)
collar	kołnierz	(kow-nyesh)
color	kolor	(ko-lor)
comb	grzebień	(gzeb-yen)
come	chodz	(hodz)
consent	pozwolenie	(poz-vo-lenye)
cook, to	gotować	(go-to-vach)
cookies	ciastka	(chast-ka)
cord	sznur	(schnoor)
corn	ziarno	(zyar-no)
cost	koszt	(kosht)
cotton	bawelna	(ba-vel-na)
cough, to	kaszlać	(kash-lach)
count, to	liczyć	(lee-cheech)
counter	kantor	(kan-tor)
cousin	kuzyn	(koo-zin)
cover, to	nakrywać	(na-kri-vach)
cow	krowa	(kro-va)
cracker	pukawka	(poo-kav-ka)
cradle	kołyska	(ko-wis-ka)
cream	krem	(krem)
crib	komora	(ko-mo-ra)
crumbs	okruch	(ok-rooh)
cry, to	płakać	(pwa-kach)
crystal	krystał	(krish-taw)
cucumber	ogórek	(o-goo-rek)

cuddle	**przytulić**	(pshi-too-leech)
cup	**garnuszek**	(gar-noo-shek)
cupboard	**szafa**	(sha-fa)
cure	**leczenie**	(le-che-nye)
curtain	**firanka**	(fee-ran-ka)
custard	**krem**	(krem)
cut, to	**krajać**	(kra-yach)
cutlet	**kotlet**	(kot-let)
dad	**tatuś**	(ta-toosh)
damp	**wilgoć**	(veel-goch)
dance, to	**tanczyć**	(tan-chich)
dark	**ćiemno**	(chem-no)
daughter	**córka**	(tsoor-ka)
daughter-in-law	**synowa**	(si-no-va)
day	**dzień**	(dzen)
dear	**drogi**	(dro-gee)
decide	**postanowić**	(pos-ta-no-veech)
decorate	**stroić**	(stro-eech)
deep	**głębia**	(gwem-bya)
deer	**sarna**	(sar-na)
defend	**bronić**	(bro-neech)
delay	**opózniać**	(o-pooz-nach)
delicious	**wyborny**	(vi-bor-ni)
dense, thick	**gęsty**	(gen-sti)
deodorize	**odwaniać**	(od-van-yach)
depend	**zalezeć**	(za-le-zech)
deserve	**zasługiwać**	(zas-woo-gee-vach)
desk	**biuro**	(byoo-ro)
dessert	**deser**	(de-ser)
destroy	**zniszczyć**	(zneesh-cheech)
detergent	**czyszczący**	(chish-chon-tsi)
diaper	**pieluszka**	(pye-lush-ka)
difficult	**trudny**	(trood-ni)
dining room	**sala jadalna**	(sa-la ya-dal-na)
dinner	**obiad**	(ob-yad)

dirty	**brudny**	(brood-ni)
discuss	**dyskutować**	(dis-koo-to-vach)
disease	**choroba**	(ho-ro-ba)
dish	**półmisek**	(poow-mee-sek)
dishes	**talerzy**	(ta-le-zee)
dishwasher	**maszyna na**	(mashee-na na)
do	**robić**	(ro-beech)
doctor	**lekarz**	(le-kaz)
dog	**pies**	(pyes)
doll	**lalka**	(lal-ka)
door	**drzwi**	(dzvee)
dough	**ciasto**	(chas-to)
down	**nadol**	(na-dol)
dozen	**tuzin**	(too-zeen)
drain	**drenować**	(dre-no-vach)
drapes	**draperja**	(dra-per-ya)
draw	**rysować**	(ri-so-vach)
dream	**sen**	(sen)
drink, to	**pić, napić**	(peech, na-peech)
drugstore	**apteka**	(ap-te-ka)
dry	**suchy**	(soo-hi)
dry cleaners	**pralnia**	(pral-nya)
dryer	**maszyna na**	(ma-shee-na na)
dry, to	**wysuszenie**	(vi-soo-she-nye)
dust	**kurz**	(kooz)
dust, to	**okurzać**	(o-koo-shach)
each	**kazdy**	(kaz-di)
ear	**ucho**	(oo-ho)
early	**wcześnie**	(vchesh-nye)
earn	**zapracować**	(za-pra-tso-vach)
egg	**jajko**	(yay-ko)
elbow	**łokieć**	(wo-kech)
empty	**prózne**	(prooz-ne)
end	**koniec**	(kon-yets)
enough	**dosyć**	(do-seech)

entertain	**zabawiać**	(za-bav-yach)
explain	**wytłumaczyć**	(vit-woo-ma-cheech)
eye	**oko**	(o-ko)
face	**twarz**	(tvaz)
far	**daleko**	(da-le-ko)
father	**ojćiec**	(oy-chets)
father-in-law	**teść**	(teshch)
faucet	**czop**	(chop)
fill, to	**napelnić**	(na-pel-neech)
finger	**palec**	(pa-lets)
finish, to	**dokonczyć**	(do-kon-cheech)
fire	**ogień**	(og-yen)
fireplace	**kominek**	(ko-mi-nek)
fish	**ryba**	(ri-ba)
fixtures (faucets)	**czopki**	(chop-kee)
floor	**podłoge**	(pod-wo-ge)
flower	**kwiat**	(kw-yat)
foot	**noga**	(no-ga)
footstool	**stoleczek**	(sto-le-chek)
fork	**widelec**	(vee-de-lets)
freeze, to	**zamarzać**	(za-mar-zach)
fresh	**swiezy**	(sh-wye-zi)
friend	**przyjaćiel**	(pshi-ya-chel)
from	**od**	(od)
front	**przód**	(pshood)
fruit	**owoce**	(o-vo-tse)
fry, to	**smarzyć**	(sma-zich)
furniture	**meble**	(meb-le)
game	**zabawa**	(za-ba-va)
garage	**garaz**	(ga-raz)
garbage	**smieći**	(shmye-chee)
garden	**ogród, sad**	(og-rood, sad)
garlic	**czosnek**	(chos-nek)

give, to	**dać**	(dach)
glass	**szkło**	(sh-kwo)
go, to	**iść**	(eeshch)
gold	**złoto**	(zwo-to)
good	**dobre, dobrze**	(dob-re, dob-ze)
grandchildren	**wnuczki**	(vnooch-kee)
grandfather	**dziadek**	(dga-dek)
grandmother	**babka, busia**	(bap-ka, boo-sha)
grapes	**winogrone**	(vee-no-gro-ne)
groceries	**towary spozy-** **wcze**	(to-va-ri spo- zeevche)
grocery store	**sklep sporzy-** **wczy**	(sklep spo-zeev-chi)
hair	**włosy**	(vwo-si)
half	**połowa**	(poo-wo-va)
hall	**sala**	(sa-la)
ham	**szynka**	(shin-ka)
hamburger	**hamburger**	(ham-boor-ger)
hammer	**mlot**	(m-lot)
hamper/basket	**kosz**	(kosh)
hand	**ręka**	(ren-ka)
handkerchief	**chustka**	(hust-ka)
hanger	**wieszadło**	(vye-shad-wo)
happy	**wesoły**	(ve-so-wi)
head	**głowa**	(gwo-va)
headache	**głowa boli**	(gwo-va bo-lee)
heavy	**cięzki**	(chen-zkee)
heel	**pięta**	(pyen-ta)
help, to	**pomagać**	(po-ma-gach)
here	**tutaj**	(too-tay)
high	**wysoko**	(vi-so-ko)
home	**dom**	(dom)
homework	**zadanie**	(za-da-nye)
honey	**miód**	(myood)
hose	**was, pończohe**	(vas, poyn-cho-he)

hot	**gorąco**	(go-ron-tso)
house	**dom**	(dom)
how	**jak**	(yak)
hunger	**głodny**	(gwod-ni)
hurry, to	**prędko**	(prend-ko)
husband	**malzonek, mąz**	(mal-zo-nek, monz)
ice	**lod**	(lod)
ice cream	**lody**	(lodi)
ill	**chory**	(ho-ri)
inside	**wnętrze**	(vnent-zhe)
iron	**zelazo**	(ze-la-zo)
iron, to	**prasować**	(pra-so-vach)
jacket	**zakiet**	(za-ket)
jelly	**powidła**	(po-veed-wa)
jewelry	**bizuterja**	(bee-zoo-ter-ya)
juice	**sok**	(sok)
kettle	**koćiel**	(ko-chel)
key	**klucz**	(klooch)
kiss, to	**pocałować**	(po-tsa-wo-vach)
kitchen	**kuchnia**	(kooh-nya)
knee	**kolano**	(ko-la-no)
knife	**nóz**	(nooz)
know, to	**wiedzieć**	(vye-dgech)
ladder	**drabina**	(dra-bee-na)
lady	**pani**	(pa-nee)
lamp	**lampa**	(lam-pa)
lampshade	**abazur**	(a-ba-zoor)
latch	**klamka**	(klam-ka)
laundry	**bielizna**	(bye-leez-na)
leather	**skóra**	(skoo-ra)
left	**lewa**	(le-va)
leg	**noga**	(no-ga)

lemon	**cytryna**	(tsit-ri-na)
letter	**list**	(leest)
lettuce	**sałata**	(sa-wa-ta)
lid	**przykrywka**	(pshi-kriv-ka)
light	**swiatło**	(sh-vyat-wo)
light, to	**oświecić**	(osh-vye-cheech)
linen	**bielizna**	(bye-leez-na)
lipstick	**pomada**	(po-ma-da)
lock up, to	**zamykać**	(za-mi-kach)
look, to	**szukać**	(shoo-kach)
loud	**głośno**	(gwosh-no)
love, to	**kochać**	(ko-hach)
lunch	**obiad**	(ob-yad)
magazine	**magazyn**	(ma-ga-zin)
mail	**poczta**	(poch-ta)
man	**mężczyzna**	(men-chiz-na)
matches	**zapałki**	(za-paw-kee)
mattress	**materac**	(ma-te-rats)
measure, to	**miarować**	(mya-ro-vach)
meat	**mięso**	(myen-so)
medicine	**lekarstwo**	(le-kar-stvo)
melon	**melon**	(me-lon)
milk	**mleko**	(mle-ko)
mirror	**lustro**	(loos-tro)
mix, to	**mieszać**	(mye-shach)
money	**pieniądze**	(pye-nyon-ze)
mop	**wiecheć**	(vye-hech)
morning	**rano**	(ra-no)
mother	**matka**	(mat-ka)
mother-in-law	**teściowa**	(tesh-cho-va)
mouth	**gęmba**	(gem-ba)
mushroom	**grzyb**	(gzib)
name	**imię, nazwisko**	(eem-ye, na-zvee-sko)

nap	drzemać	(dze-mach)
napkin	serwetka	(ser-vet-ka)
near	blisko	(blees-ko)
neck	szyja	(shi-ya)
need, to	potrzeba	(pot-she-ba)
needle	igła	(eeg-wa)
neighbor	sąsiad	(son-shad)
nephew	bratanek	(bra-ta-nek)
never	nigdy	(neeg-di)
new	nowy	(no-vi)
newspaper	gazeta	(ga-ze-ta)
niece	śiostrzenica	(shos-tze-nee-tsa)
night	noc	(nots)
nobody	nikt	(neekt)
noise	hałas	(ha-was)
noon	południe	(po-wood-nye)
nose	nos	(nos)
now	teras	(te-ras)
nut	orzech	(osheh)
nutmeg	muszkat	(moos-kat)
obey	usłuchać	(oos-woo-hach)
o'clock	godzina	(go-zee-na)
oil	oliwa	(o-lee-va)
old	stary	(sta-ri)
olives	oliwka	(o-leev-ka)
onion	cebula	(tse-boo-la)
open, to	otworzyć	(ot-vo-zeech)
orange	pomarańcza	(po-ma-ran-cha)
out, go	wychodzić	(vi-ho-dzeech)
oven	piec	(pyets)
pail	wiadro	(vyad-ro)
pan	patelnia	(pa-tel-nya)
paper	papier	(pap-yer)
parsley	pietruszka	(pyet-roosh-ka)

pear	**gruszka**	(groosh-ka)
peas	**groszek**	(gro-shek)
pen	**pióro**	(pyoo-ro)
pepper	**piepsz**	(pyepsh)
piano	**fortepian**	(for-te-pyan)
piano keys	**klawiatura**	(kla-vya-too-ra)
picture	**obraz**	(ob-raz)
pie	**placek**	(pla-tsek)
piece	**kawałek**	(ka-va-wek)
pillow	**poduszka**	(po-doosh-ka)
pillowcase	**poszywka**	(po-shiv-ka)
pin	**szpilka**	(sh-peel-ka)
pineapple	**ananas**	(a-na-nas)
plate	**talerz**	(ta-lez)
play, to	**bawić**	(ba-veech)
poison	**trucizna**	(troo-cheez-na)
polish, to	**polerowac**	(po-le-ro-vach)
polish (noun)	**połysk**	(po-wisk)
poor	**biedny**	(byed-ni)
pork	**wieprzowina**	(vye-psho-vee-na)
pot	**garnek**	(gar-nek)
potato	**ziemńiak**	(zyem-nyak)
pound	**funt**	(foont)
powder	**proszek**	(pro-shek)
pretty	**piękna**	(pyen-kna)
purse	**sakiewka**	(sak-yev-ka)
put, to	**połorzyc**	(po-wo-zhich)
quart	**kwarta**	(kvar-ta)
quarter	**ćwierć**	(chvyerch)
question	**pytanie**	(pi-ta-nye)
quickly	**prędko**	(pren-dko)
quiet	**ćicho**	(chee-ho)
quilt	**kołdra**	(kow-dra)
quit	**przestać**	(pshes-tach)

radish	**rzodkiewka**	(zhod-kyev-ka)
rag	**szmata**	(shma-ta)
rain	**deszcz**	(deshch)
raisin	**rodynek**	(ro-di-nek)
raspberry	**malina**	(ma-lee-na)
rattle	**turkot**	(toor-kot)
raw	**surowy**	(soo-ro-vi)
red	**czerwony**	(cher-vo-ni)
refrigerator	**lodówka**	(lo-doov-ka)
remember, to	**pamiętać**	(pam-yen-tach)
rest, to	**spoczywać**	(spo-chi-vach)
ribbon	**wstązka**	(vston-shka)
rich	**bogaty**	(bo-ga-ti)
right	**prawo**	(pra-vo)
ring	**pierścionek**	(pyer-shcho-nek)
rinse, to	**płókać**	(pwoo-kach)
room	**pokój**	(po-kooy)
rotten	**zgnite**	(z-gnee-te)
round	**koło, dokoła**	(ko-wo, do-ko-wa)
rug	**dywan**	(di-van)
safety pin	**szpilka**	(sh-peel-ka)
salad	**sałata**	(sa-wa-ta)
sale	**sprzedaz**	(spshe-daz)
salt	**sól**	(sool)
sandwich	**kanapka**	(ka-nap-ka)
sauce	**sos**	(sos)
sausage	**kielbasa**	(kyel-ba-sa)
school	**szkoła**	(shko-wa)
scissors	**narzecki**	(na-shech-kee)
scrambled (eggs)	**ubijane (jajka)**	(oo-bee-ya-ne yayka)
seed	**naśienie**	(na-shen-ye)
servant	**słuzący**	(swoo-zon-sti)
sew, to	**szyć**	(sheech)

sheets	**prześcieradło**	(pshesh-che-rad-wo)
shelf	**półka**	(poow-ka)
shirt	**koszula**	(ko-shoo-la)
shoes	**trzewiki**	(tshe-vee-kee)
short	**krutki**	(kroot-kee)
shower	**tusz, tuszym**	(toosh, too-shim)
shrimp	**raczek**	(ra-chek)
sick	**chory**	(ho-ri)
side	**strona**	(stro-na)
silk	**jedwab**	(yed-vab)
silver	**śrebro**	(shreb-ro)
sink	**ściek**	(sh-chek)
size	**miara**	(mya-ra)
skillet	**patelnia**	(pa-tel-nya)
slacks	**spodnie**	(spod-nye)
sleep, to	**spać**	(spach)
slow	**pomało**	(po-ma-wo)
slowly	**pomałúsko**	(po-ma-woosh-ko)
smoke	**dym**	(dim)
smoke, to	**palić**	(pa-leech)
soap	**mydło**	(mid-wo)
sofa	**kanapa**	(ka-na-pa)
soft	**miękki**	(myen-kee)
some	**jakiś**	(ya-keesh)
something	**coś**	(tsosh)
son	**syn**	(sin)
son-in-law	**synowy**	(si-no-vi)
soon	**zaraz**	(za-raz)
spice	**przyprawa**	(pshi-pra-va)
spinach	**szpinak**	(shpee-nak)
sponge	**gąbka**	(gomp-ka)
spoon	**łyzka**	(wish-ka)
sprinkle, to	**kropić**	(kro-peech)
starch	**krochmal**	(kroh-mal)
starch, to	**krochmalić**	(kroh-ma-leech)

steak	**befsztyk**	(bef-shtik)
steam	**para**	(pa-ra)
stockings	**pończochy**	(pon-cho-hi)
stomach	**zołądek**	(zo-won-dek)
stopper	**kurek**	(koo-rek)
stove	**piec**	(pyets)
straight	**prosto**	(pros-to)
street	**ulica**	(oo-lee-tsa)
sugar	**cuker**	(tsoo-ker)
suit	**garnitur**	(gar-nee-toor)
suitcase	**torepka**	(to-rep-ka)
sweep	**zmiatać**	(zmya-tach)
swim	**pływać**	(pli-vach)
table	**stól**	(stool)
little table	**stolik**	(sto-leek)
take	**brać**	(brach)
taste, to	**smakować**	(sma-ko-vach)
tea	**harbata**	(har-ba-ta)
tears	**łzy**	(wzi)
teeth	**zęby**	(zen-bi)
television	**telewizja**	(te-le-veez-ya)
there	**tam**	(tam)
thimble	**naparstek**	(na-par-stek)
thing	**rzecz**	(shech)
thread	**nitka**	(neet-ka)
throat	**gardło**	(gard-wo)
tile	**kafle**	(ka-fle)
toast	**pszypiekać**	(pshi-pye-kach)
toilet	**tualeta**	(twa-le-ta)
tomato	**pomidor**	(po-mee-dor)
tongue	**język**	(yen-zik)
tooth	**ząb**	(zomb)
toothache	**ból zębów**	(bool zen-boov)
towel	**ręcznik**	(rench-neek)
toy	**zabawa**	(za-ba-va)

trash	**śmiecie**	(shmye-che)
travel, to	**podróz**	(pod-rooz)
tree	**drzewo**	(dge-vo)
trousers	**portki**	(port-kee)
turkey	**indyk**	(een-dik)
turnip	**rzepa**	(she-pa)
umbrella	**parasol**	(pa-ra-sol)
under	**pod**	(pod)
underneath	**pod spodem**	(pod spo-dem)
up	**wysoko**	(vi-so-ko)
use, to	**urzywać**	(oo-shi-vach)
vacuum cleaner	**maszyna na dywan**	(ma-shi-na na di-van)
valuable	**wartosćiowy**	(var-tosh-cho-vi)
vanilla	**wanilja**	(va-neel-ya)
vase	**wazon**	(va-zon)
veal	**cielęćina**	(che-len-chee-na)
vegetables	**jarzyny**	(ya-shi-ni)
very	**bardzo**	(bar-dzo)
vinegar	**ocet**	(o-tset)
vitamin	**witamina**	(vee-ta-mee-na)
voice	**głos**	(gwos)
wait, to	**poczekać**	(po-che-kach)
walk, to	**chodzić**	(ho-dzeech)
wall	**ściana**	(shcha-na)
wallet	**bilet**	(bee-let)
wash, to	**wymyć**	(vi-mich)
washing machine	**pralka**	(pral-ka)
wastebasket	**kosz na smieći**	(kosh na shmye-che)
watch	**zegarek**	(ze-ga-rek)
water	**woda**	(vo-da)

watermelon	**arbuz**	(ar-booz)
wax	**wosk**	(vosk)
weather	**pogoda**	(po-go-da)
wedding	**wesele**	(ve-se-le)
week	**tydzień**	(ti-dgyen)
welcome	**powitanie**	(po-vee-ta-nye)
wet	**mokre**	(mok-re)
when	**kiedy**	(kye-di)
where	**gdzie**	(gdze)
while	**chociasz**	(ho-chash)
white	**biały**	(bya-wi)
why	**czemu**	(che-moo)
wide	**szeroko**	(she-ro-ko)
wife	**rzona**	(zo-na)
window	**okno**	(ok-no)
wine	**wino**	(vee-no)
woman	**kobieta**	(ko-bye-ta)
wool	**welna**	(vel-na)
work	**praca**	(pra-tsa)
yellow	**zołty**	(zoow-ti)
yesterday	**wczoraj**	(vcho-ray)
young	**młody**	(mwo-di)